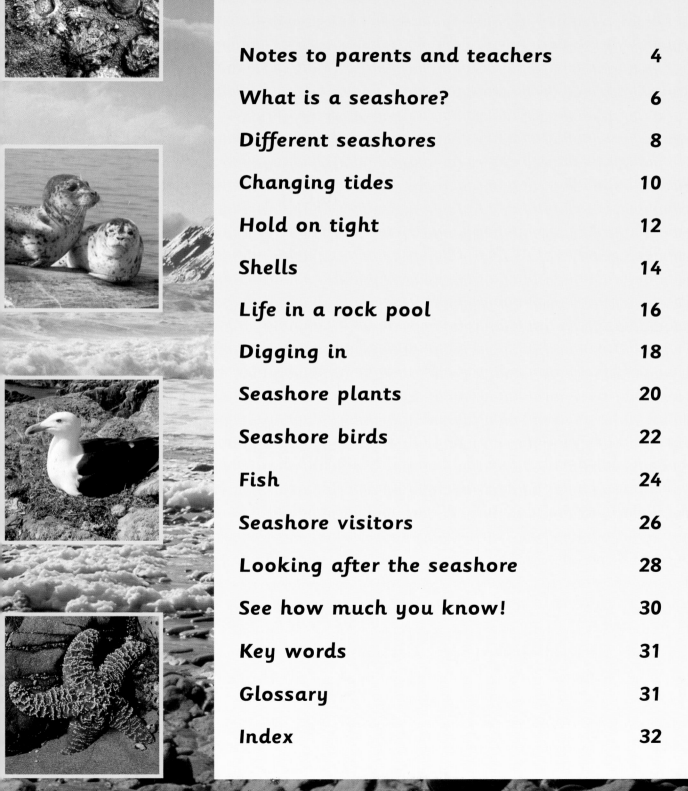

CONTENTS

Notes to parents and teachers

This series has been developed for group use in the classroom as well as for children reading on their own. In particular, its differentiated text allows children of mixed abilities to enjoy reading about the same topic. The larger size text (A, below) offers apprentice readers a simplified text. This simplified text is used in the introduction to each chapter and in the picture captions. This font is part of the © Sassoon family of fonts recommended by the National Literacy Early Years Strategy document for maximum legibility. The smaller size text (B, below) offers a more challenging read for older or more able readers.

Fish

At low tide, seashore fish hide. They squeeze into cracks in rock pools or hide under the sand.

 A

◀ **This fish lives in rock pools.**

Goby fish live in rock pools. Their skin is patterned to help them hide against the rocks.

B

Questions, key words and glossary

Each spread ends with a question which parents and teachers can use to discuss and develop further ideas and concepts. Further questions are provided in a quiz on page 30. A reduced version of pages 30 and 31 is shown below. The illustrated 'Key words' section is provided as a revision tool, particularly for apprentice readers, in order to help with spelling, writing and guided reading as part of the literacy hour. The glossary is for more able or older readers. In addition to the glossary's role as a reference aid, it is also designed to reinforce new vocabulary and provide a tool for further discussion and revision. When glossary terms first appear in the text, they are highlighted in bold.

 ### See how much you know!

Which animal leaves a squiggly pile of sand on the beach?

What do turtles do when they visit the seashore?

What do seashore fish do at low tide?

What is the sand on a sandy beach made from?

Why do sea otters wrap themselves in seaweed?

Which rock pool animal can grow new arms?

Why do seabirds have different shaped beaks?

Key words

Hermit crab

A

Beach
Cliff
Fish   Waves

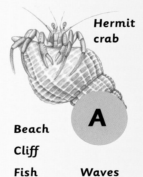

Seaweed

Glossary

Colonies – A group of the same kind of animals or plants living together.
Estuary – Where a river meets the sea or ocean. There is a mixture of freshwater and saltwater in an estuary.
Food chain – Limpets eat seaweed and dog whelks eat limpets. So, the seaweed, limpets and dog whelks form a food chain. They rely on each other for food.
Gravity – The pulling force between two large objects. The Moon's gravity pulls the Earth's oceans and seas to cause tides.

B

Habitat — The place in which a plant or animal lives.
Predator – A flesh-eating animal.
Rootlets – A small root. Some seaweeds have rootlets to hold on to rocks.

30

31

5

What is a seashore?

The seashore is where the land meets the sea. Sometimes seashores are rocky and have high cliffs. Other seashores are gently sloping, sandy beaches. In some places seashores are made from lots of smooth stones.

◀ **These waves are crashing against cliffs.**

This seashore is made from hard rock and has steep cliffs. When waves smash against the cliffs, they slowly wear them away or crack the rock. Sometimes the cliff breaks apart and large pieces of rock fall down into the sea. Under the water, the fallen rocks are tumbled together by the waves and break up into tiny pieces.

▶ A sandy beach slopes down into the sea.

When land made from soft rocks meets the sea, the seashore is flat and sandy. Sand is made up of billions of tiny pieces of rock and broken shells.

Shingle beaches are covered with stones.

Shingle beaches are made up of small pebbles that have been smoothed by the waves. Shingle seashores are hard places for animals and plants to live because the sea moves the stones around. Most wildlife lives high up on the shore out of reach of the waves.

 Which kind of seashore would be the best home for animals?

Different seashores

There are different seashores all over the world. Some seashores are hot and some are icy cold. The animals found on an icy seashore can live where it is very cold. They keep warm by having thick fur or oily feathers and a layer of fat under their skin.

◄ **These birds are looking for food in the mud.**

When rivers reach the sea they spread out into a wide, muddy seashore called an **estuary**. Huge flocks of birds feed on muddy estuaries. They hunt for worms, shellfish or crabs in the mud. When the sea flows into the estuary and covers the mud, the birds fly ashore and wait until it goes out again.

◀ These penguins live on a cold, icy seashore.

In very cold parts of the world, the seashore is icy. Penguins nest on the icy seashores of the Antarctic. It is so cold that they huddle together to keep warm. They keep their egg on top of their feet to stop it from freezing on the ice.

This seashore is in a hot part of the world.

Coral reefs grow in warm, shallow seas. Coral reefs are made by small animals that live close together. They protect themselves by building hard cases. It is the hard cases that form the coral reef. Coral reefs are important because they are home to many animals.

Sea

Island

Coral reef

Coral reef

 How would you survive on a freezing, icy seashore?

Changing tides

Twice a day, the sea moves up and down the seashore. It is high tide when the beach is covered with sea. After high tide, the sea turns and goes back out again. When the sea is far out and the beach is uncovered, it is low tide.

▼ **At high tide the seashore is covered.**

At high tide, the seashore is covered with water. The high tide line is the highest place the water reaches up the seashore. The tides are caused by the **gravity** of the Moon and Sun pulling the seawater towards them.

 The seashore is uncovered at low tide.

At low tide, the seashore is uncovered and the sea is far out. On some seashores the difference between high and low tides is big. On others it is small. Low tide happens twice in about 25 hours.

Waves are made by the wind.

The waves that move across the sea and break on a seashore are made by the wind. When the wind blows over the sea, it pushes and drags against the surface and forms waves. Strong storm winds make huge waves. On days when there is no wind blowing, the sea is calm and the waves are very small.

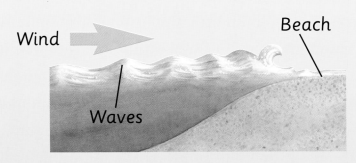

Wind

Beach

Waves

 How are tides and waves different?

Hold on tight

The waves that crash on to a seashore are very strong. Seashore plants and animals must hold on tight to keep themselves safe. If they let go, they could be washed away or smashed on the rocks.

◀ **These limpets are holding on to a rock.**

Seashore animals have different ways of holding on. Limpets use their strong foot to grip tightly on to rocks and stop them from being washed away. Some animals, like sea urchins, cling on to rocks with lots of tiny feet that look like tubes. Mussel shellfish anchor themselves down to rocks with tough threads.

This seaweed grips on tightly to the rocks.

Seaweeds anchor themselves on to rocks to stop them from being washed away by strong waves. Large seaweeds grip on to rocks with strong, finger-like **rootlets** called holdfasts. During storms, seaweed is ripped off rocks.

Sea otters wrap themselves in seaweed.

When sea otters sleep, they wrap themselves in giant kelp seaweed. They grab a floating end of kelp and spin around in the water. The kelp wraps around the otter and anchors it down. It stops the sea from carrying the sea otter away in its sleep.

? Can you think of other animals or plants that hold on tight?

Shells

Shellfish are small animals that live inside shells. Their hard shells help to keep them safe from being eaten by other animals or smashed by waves. When shellfish are out of water (left), their shells stop them from drying out.

◀ **These shellfish live in one shell.**

Some shellfish live in one shell. The animal that lives inside has a very strong, muscular foot which it uses to move itself and to cling to rocks with. If the animal is in danger, it withdraws and hides inside its shell. These shellfish feed on seaweed or on other animals.

◀ This shellfish has two shells joined together.

Some shellfish have two shells that are hinged together. Scallop shellfish swim by flapping their shells open and shut. Shellfish with two shells feed by sucking in water, and straining out small bits of food.

This hermit crab lives in an old shell.

Hermit crabs have a long soft body which they protect by living in an empty shell. They have a pair of strong hooks on their rear end to hold them safely in their shell. When a hermit crab grows too big for its shell, it will find a bigger shell to live in.

Hermit crab

Whelk shell

 What other animals have a shell to protect them?

Life in a rock pool

When the tide goes out, some water is left behind in hollows in the rocks. Many different seaweeds and animals live in these rock pools. They can stay safely underwater in the rock pool until the sea comes in again.

◄ **Starfish live in rock pools.**

The underside of a starfish is covered with lots of tiny tube feet. It uses the feet to move and to grip on to rocks. Starfish feed on shellfish and use their arms to force open the shells to reach the soft animal inside. If a starfish loses any of its arms, it can grow new ones.

▶ Sea anemones are animals.

Sea anemones look like flowers, but they are animals. They catch food with their tentacles. When a sea anemone is out of the water, it pulls in its tentacles to stop itself from drying out. It looks like a blob of jelly!

Limpets eat seaweed.

Seaweed

Limpet

Dog whelks eat limpets.

Dog whelk

This is a rock pool food chain.

A **food chain** shows the link between plants and animals in a **habitat**. All food chains start with plants, which are eaten by plant-eating animals. Plant-eaters are eaten by flesh-eating animals. In a rock pool, seaweeds are food for animals like limpets. Limpets are eaten by whelks.

 How do rock pools protect plants and animals?

Digging in

Many seashore animals bury themselves in the sand, mud or rock. They dig themselves in to try to keep themselves safe from being eaten. Some animals hide in the sand when the tide is out. This stops the animal from drying out in the wind or Sun.

◄ These are lugworm casts on a sandy beach.

Lugworms live in U-shaped burrows on sandy or muddy seashores. They swallow mud and eat any pieces of food they find in it. The sand comes out of the worms' bottom at the other end of the burrow, and makes a squiggly worm cast on the surface of the mud.

▲ **This dog whelk hides in cracks in rocks.**

Some shellfish protect themselves by digging into rock or squeezing into gaps between rocks. Dog whelks hide under rocks, crawl into cracks and wedge themselves into crevices on rocky seashores when the tide goes out. When the tide comes back in the dog whelks come out to feed.

Cockles bury themselves in the sand.

Cockles use their muscular foot to bury themselves in the sand. This helps to protect them from being eaten by birds and animals. Cockles and razorshells feed using long **siphons** that suck water and strain food from it.

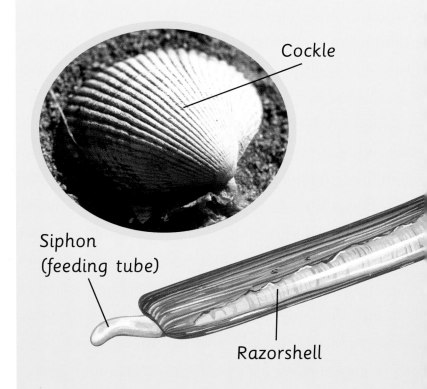

Cockle

Siphon (feeding tube)

Razorshell

 Where do seashore animals hide? Why?

Seashore plants

Many plants live on the seashore. Seaweeds are seashore plants that can live in salty seawater. Some seashore plants can only live on the land. They grow high up the shore, out of the reach of the waves.

◀ **This seaweed floats in the water.**

Bladder wrack seaweed has pockets of air and jelly to help it float in the water. Its tough leathery leaves are covered in a slippery, gummy substance to protect it from drying out at low tide. Bladder wrack can survive out of water while the tide is out.

▶ Kelp seaweed grows very fast.

Californian kelp seaweed is the fastest growing plant in the world. It can grow up to one metre in a day and can reach lengths of 100 metres. Kelp grows in huge underwater forests, which are home to many fish and other animals.

These tough grasses grow on sand dunes.

Marram grass is a tough plant that grows on sand dunes at the seashore. It has thin, curled leaves to protect it from drying out in the wind and the Sun. Marram grass has long roots to reach down to water. The roots stop the plant blowing away.

Beach

Marram grass roots

 Where can seashore plants grow?

Seashore birds

Seashore birds feed on different foods. They hunt for food on the land and in the sea. Some birds dig in the sand to find worms and shellfish. Fish-eating birds dive into the sea to catch their food.

◀ **Seashore birds build their nests on steep cliffs.**

Seashore birds often nest together in huge, noisy **colonies**. They make their nests on high, rocky cliffs because it is very difficult for **predators** to reach them there. Some seabirds make nests, but others just lay their eggs on a rocky ledge.

These birds feed on shellfish, fish and tiny animals.

Each type of seashore bird has a beak that is the perfect size and shape for finding and catching its food.

Avocet

An avocet has a long, curved beak for catching shrimps and insects. It sweeps its beak from side to side, and strains tiny animals from the water.

Cormorant

Birds that dive into the water to catch fish, such as this cormorant, have long, sharp, dagger-like beaks.

Oystercatcher

Oystercatchers eat shellfish. They have a long, thin beak that they use to open shells.

Turnstones eat animals that live under stones and seaweed. They use their short beak to push stones and seaweed aside to hunt for food.

Turnstone

 What do you think are the dangers of nesting on a cliff?

Fish

At low tide, seashore fish hide. They squeeze into cracks in rock pools or hide under the sand. When the tide comes in, they come out to feed. Seashore fish have eyes near the top of their head. They look out for seabirds that try to catch them from above.

◀ This fish lives in rock pools.

Goby fish live in rock pools. Their skin is patterned to help them hide against the rocks and seaweed. Some goby fish have their lower fins joined together to make a sucker. They use the sucker to cling on to rocks and stop them from being swept away by waves.

These pipefish are hard to see.

Pipefish can hide themselves so well that they are very hard to see. They have a long, thin body that helps to disguise them when they hide in seaweed. They live in rock pools and feed on other small fish and shellfish.

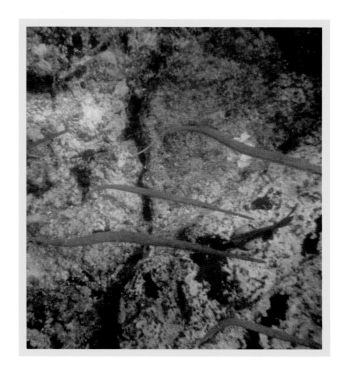

This fish can breathe air.

Mudskipper fish live on warm, muddy seashores. Most fish can only breathe in water. Mudskipper fish can breathe in air and water. They use their front fins as legs and crawl about on mud to look for food.

 What types of fish can you name?

Seashores visitors

Some of the animals that we see on a seashore do not live there all the time. They spend most of their life in the sea, and only visit the seashore for a short time. They may visit the shore to rest or to have babies.

◄ **These seals have come to the shore to rest.**

Seals spend most of their time in the sea, but they sometimes visit the seashore. Seals are excellent swimmers but move very slowly on land. They haul themselves up on to rocks or sand banks to rest and bask in the Sun. Seals give birth to their pups on quiet seashores where they will not be disturbed.

Puffins visit the seashore to nest.

Puffins visit the seashore each year to breed. They nest on the top of cliffs. They dig burrows or take over an old rabbit tunnel. Puffins usually have only one chick. They feed their chicks on sand eels and fish.

Turtles visit the shore to lay their eggs.

Female turtles come ashore at night to lay their eggs above the high tide line. They dig a hole in the sand, lay their eggs in it and cover the eggs with sand. When the babies hatch, they dig themselves out and crawl down to the sea.

 Why do you think puffins dig a burrow to nest in?

Looking after the seashore

Seashores can be harmed by people. If we leave rubbish on a beach, it can hurt or kill wildlife. Plants and animals often lose their homes when we build on the seashore. We all need to take care of the seashore and the wildlife that lives there.

◀ This rubbish has been washed up on a beach.

Rubbish is often dumped in the sea. It can be carried long distances and washed up on beaches. Rubbish like plastic bottles and bags, fishing line and glass can hurt or kill animals. Turtles eat plastic bags because they look like jellyfish.

▶ This bird is covered in oil.

When oil is spilled from ships at sea it can wash ashore. Oil can clog seabirds' feathers so they cannot fly. It also stops them from being waterproof, so they get wet and cold. When they try to clean themselves they swallow the oil. Oil can kill many of the living things on a seashore.

This seashore is cared for to keep the wildlife safe.

Some seashores have been made into nature reserves to protect them. This stops seashores from being changed by people. Making seashores into nature reserves keeps the animals and plants that live there safe.

 How could you help to take care of a seashore?

See how much you know!

Which animal leaves a squiggly pile of sand on the beach?

What do turtles do when they visit the seashore?

What do seashore fish do at low tide?

What is the sand on a sandy beach made from?

Why do sea otters wrap themselves in seaweed?

Which rock pool animal can grow new arms?

Why do seabirds have different shaped beaks?

Key words

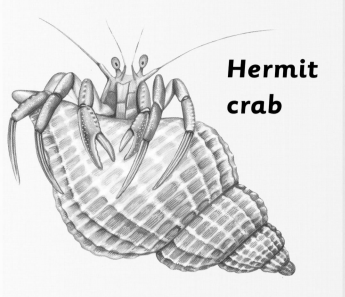

Hermit crab

Beach **Nest** **Shell**

Cliff **Rock** **Tide**

Fish **Sand** **Waves**

Seaweed

Glossary

Colonies – A group of the same kind of animals or plants living together.

Estuary – Where a river meets the sea or ocean. There is a mixture of freshwater and saltwater in an estuary.

Food chain – Limpets eat seaweed and dog whelks eat limpets. So, the seaweed, limpets and dog whelks form a food chain. They rely on each other for food.

Gravity – The pulling force between two large objects. The Moon's gravity pulls the Earth's oceans and seas to cause tides.

Habitat – The place in which a plant or animal lives.

Predator – A flesh-eating animal.

Rootlet – A small root. Some seaweeds have rootlets to hold on to rocks.

Siphon – A long tube through which some animals feed.

Index

Seashores

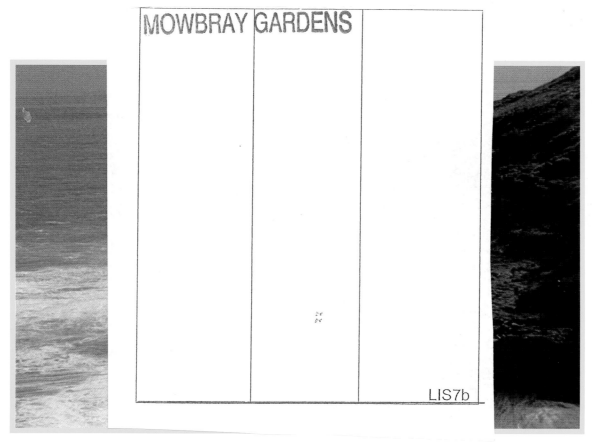

Aladdin/Watts
London • Sydney

PAPERBACK EDITION PRINTED 2007

© Aladdin Books Ltd 2004

Designed and produced by
Aladdin Books Ltd
2/3 Fitzroy Mews
London W1T 6DF

First published in 2004 by
Franklin Watts
338 Euston Road
London NW1 3BH

Franklin Watts Australia
Level 17/207 Kent Street
Sydney NSW 2000

Franklin Watts is a division of
Hachette Children's Books

ISBN 978 0 7496 7757 2

A catalogue record for this
book is available from the
British Library.

Dewey Classification:
577.69

Editor:
Harriet Brown

Designers:
Flick, Book Design and Graphics
Simon Morse

Picture Researcher:
Brian Hunter Smart

Literacy consultant:
Jackie Holderness – former Senior
Lecturer in Primary Education,
Westminster Institute of Education,
Oxford Brookes University

Printed in Malaysia